A IS FOR ACTION
The ABC's of Taking Action

 **Publishing**

© 2012 ED-ucation Publishing
5114 South Ridge Drive, Kelowna BC. V1W 4Y5. Canada
Visit our website at *http://www.ed-ucation.ca*

Illustrated by Jenna Cumbers   Designed by Janet Hannah

978-0-9918854-0-4 (ebook)   978-0-9918854-1-1 (paperback)

Praise for *A is for Action*

A is for Action is an amazing book that inspires us to make a difference. By using simple guidelines, **A is for Action** teaches us HOW to take sustainable action that can change our world for the better.
Kaitlyn Fox is an International Baccalaureate student, and the creator of www.IBLearnerProfile.com

This book serves a critical purpose in the education of every child, starting at the youngest age group. The concept of service and action builds empathy and gives insight into the broader human condition. Future leaders need this capacity in order to see beyond the confines of their own reality. The value of this book in guiding the process of building future compassionate global leadership is enormous.
Dr. Chris Müller is an International Baccalaureate School Director and has worked with schools in Africa, Europe and North America to develop future global leaders by fostering international-mindedness within learning communities around the world

A is for Action is a wonderful way to introduce young people to the belief that they are capable of making a difference in their community and world. The authors lead students through exercises that teach them how to formulate questions, become knowledgeable and empathize with others to understand that it is within their power to foster change.
A is for Action is engaging and inspiring.
Laurence Levine, Co-Founder and Director of Kids Can Make A Difference® (KIDS)

This isn't another book of ABC's. **A is for Action: The ABC's of Taking Action** is an excellent guide that takes every child through a practical journey of learning through action. The book exposes children to critical thinking processes that teach them how to take action to make their communities a better place.
Ghulam M. Isaczai, Chief of Development Division, UN Volunteers, is working for the United Nations fighting poverty and has been promoting sustainable development programmes around the world for the past two decades

This A to Z book, **A is for Action**, gives an overview of how kids can develop skills that lead to taking action. Across the globe, children and teens are showing their ability to transform ideas into realities that assist our communities. Young people, with the assistance of supportive adults, are indeed changing the world!
Cathryn Berger Kaye, M.A., International Consultant and Author, The Complete Guide to Service Learning

There is never a lack of willingness among children and young people when it comes to taking action and making things happen. With so many issues out there that could use the fresh eyes and the great creativity that youth bring to the table, where does one begin? **A is for Action** is a great How-To Guide to help young activists get started, providing them with the necessary tools and systematic approaches to bring positive change to their communities.
Etienne Leue, Social and Civic Media Section of UNICEF, Content Manager of Voices of Youth

"Be the change you want to see in the world."

Mahatma Gandhi

Flip back to the cover right now. What do you see? What problems can you identify? The world has problems such as poverty, pollution, war, and natural disasters. What possible solutions are offered for these problems? What other solutions can you brainstorm? What can you do to take action and be the change you want to see in the world?

AUTHOR'S NOTE:

AUTHOR'S NOTE:

Many people think that action is easy to define. It is something you do, right? But action is much more than that. Action is a part of who we are. If we want to change the world we need to start with changing ourselves. But sometimes change is hard. How do we make changes in the way we think so we can help the world? This book will help you develop ideas and skills so you can start to take action today!

STUDENTS:

Have you ever thought, "I wish I could make a difference in the world?" Good news! You are never too young to take meaningful action and make a difference in and to the world. Have you ever had someone smile and greet you in a friendly way? Did it brighten your day? That small action made a difference in your life. You have the power to make a difference too!

PARENTS:

If we want children to make a difference in the world we need to help them personalise the action they take, and understand that it is not just a mandate from their teachers and parents, but a life-long mindset they develop. The authors of this book want to challenge children to look beyond action as a one-time thing, and begin to view it as an extension of their learning and interests. Taking action can happen at any age. It's all about how we as parents, teachers, and the community, support children and youth as they begin the learning journey towards becoming adults who are agents of change!

TEACHERS:

Every teacher wants their students to take meaningful action. This book was created because the authors believe that the concept of action is more a state of mind than a product. Action can only make a resonating difference to and in the world when it is developed in conjunction with a toolbox of explicitly taught skills, modeled behaviors, scaffolded plans and a gradual release of responsibility.

Use this book in tandem with the complementary free Action Phase document which is hosted at *www.helptakeaction.com*. This resource enables teachers to implement a program that further explores the concepts within this book. It provides scaffolded learning experiences that help students gain the skills and knowledge to take sustained and meaningful action.

ACTION

Taking Action requires us to get involved,
to find a conflict or problem that we can help solve.

Taking Action goes beyond donating coins or bills,
we need to change how we think, and develop the right skills.

As you go through this book, apply what you learn.
You can make a difference, let's get started, it's your turn.

PULL

A

BELIEVE
IN YOURSELF

In order to take action, you must Believe that you can.
The biggest breakthroughs in history, this is how they began.

It all starts with one person, so ask yourself then:
If not you, then whom? If not now, then when?

Be the best you can be to positively shape the world.
Anyone can, no matter what age, boy or girl.

B

CHANGE

If you want to make a Change,
let me give you a clue,

At the end of the day,
it all starts with **YOU**.

Find a cause or a conflict
that you are passionate about,

Find a personal connection
and you are on the right route.

The more that you care
about this conflict,

the more you'll be motivated
to Change what you picked.

DISCUSS
PROBLEMS AND CONCERNS

Now that you've chosen a problem to explore,
it's time to discuss this with friends, family and more.

Begin to expand your knowledge base,
by discussing why this problem even takes place.

What is the problem and how did it start?
How is it like others? What sets them apart?

Where and when does it happen, what can you infer?
Discuss possible reasons why this problem occurs.

D

As you continue to explore,
new things you'll reveal,
but remember the importance
of how others feel.

Put yourself in the shoes of the people in need.
Consider their experience before you proceed.

Identify with them and what they go through,
to expand on what you already knew.

E

FORMULATE QUESTIONS

As you begin to explore your conflict,
let me offer a suggestion.
It is much easier to research
if you begin with a question.

The key is not to start with any old one,
Formulate Questions that are open
and you've already begun.

An open question
can not be answered with no or yes,
it requires an explanation
that goes beyond a simple guess.

Ask: who? what? when?
why? how? and where?
Just asking these questions
shows that you care.

F

SET GOALS

As you continue, keep the end in mind.
If you set goals, success you will find.

Make a detailed plan of the steps you will take,
ask who will be involved and how they'll partake.

Set goals that are clear and a definite deadline
to fulfill what you plan, and all will be fine.

There are times you may stumble and it may seem like an uphill hike.
But continue to ask yourself: "What will success look like?"

Once you have a deep sense that something is wrong,
go beyond feeling sorry, it's time to be strong.

If you even have an inkling of what you might do,
put your plan into motion and make sure to follow through.

Anyone can feel bad about another's situation,
but you, yes **YOU**, can help, if you show dedication.

INQUIRE

You've developed some goals,
and you have a great plan.
You're ready to help
and you believe that you can.

Now you're ready to explore a topic,
it's time to get going.
You must inquire into what it is
you are interested in knowing.

It is time to use those questions
that are open and wise,
to guide you to answers
that are truth and not lies.

To be sure, you must ensure
to use more than one source.
Gain multiple perspectives
and you'll be on the right course.

JOIN ORGANIZATIONS

As you ask questions, remember that you are not alone. Join others who share the same vision and your efforts have grown.

Build a network with others concerned about a similar issue, you'll appreciate new perspectives and they'll value your's too.

Disability

Join organizations and your voice will grow. There is power in numbers, so share what you know.

J

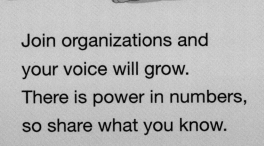

BECOME KNOWLEDGEABLE

You've already formulated questions
and inquired a lot,
but it never hurts to be more knowledgeable,
to improve what you've got.

It's important to learn
as much as you can,
about the topic and issue,
again and again.

But that's not the only thing
to learn more about,
you must gain knowledge
on how you can help out.

Consider the options
and the best reaction,
and the process itself,
of **HOW** to take action.

K

As you use interviews
to help gain more information,
ensure that you think
about effective communication.

LISTEN

There's a difference between
the words "listen" and "hear",
Take care to ensure
that their meaning is clear.

It is okay to agree
or disagree as you may,
but keep an open-mind
to what others will say.

It's essential to understand
all differing perspectives,
it's your job to investigate,
just like a detective.

L

MAKE CONNECTIONS

It's time to make connections, with what you've learned along the way.
So ask yourself these questions and reflect on what they say:

How do you connect with your topic and what is your aim?
Can you relate your topic to others? How are they different or the same?

Make connections that are local and within your community,
but also think globally, to create equal opportunity.

As you're gathering research,
please keep in mind,
it's essential to take notes
and record what you find.

TAKE

NOTES

If you use others' ideas
that are not originally from you,
ensure you give credit,
where credit is due.

If you get information from a
website, book, or interview,
don't plagiarize, cite sources,
it shows appreciation too.

N

ORGANIZE

Taking notes can get messy, so organize what you collect.
Choose a way that is helpful, what will you select?

Organization can be applied in more than one way,
keep yourself organized to help you day by day.

Use schedules and deadlines to manage your time,
use 'To Do' lists and checklists, and you'll do just fine.

You also may choose to organize an event,
collaborating together, great ideas you'll invent.

You've asked so many questions,
you've shown that you care.
You've gained so much knowledge,
now it's time that you share.

Don't limit your sharing
to just what you know,
share a solution, what to do,
and how others can grow.

Start by writing letters to the media
and members of governments,
then move online, make a case,
and back it up with evidence.

QUESTION

You've seen this before and I think you now know,
how important questioning is in order to grow.

Your action is important, so continue to try
to create **new and insightful** questions. Ask: how? and why?

Dig deeper. Go further. You may find something new
to build upon your action and what you previously knew.

REFLECT

Take a moment to Reflect on the journey you've had,
the differences you've made - I'm sure that you're glad.

Reflect on the process of how to take action,
on the skills you've developed to reach satisfaction.

Have your research and questions helped you to act?
Have you resolved the conflict? What was the impact?

R

SUSTAIN

You've had a great start and you should be proud of what you've done,
but most conflicts and battles are not so easily won.

You must endure, to ensure that your action will go on,
that your solution sustains for others to act upon.

You want it to continue to the future and never be gone,
to make a better world for your kids, their kids, and beyond.

TAKE RISKS

To sustain your action,
there are risks you must take,
to sacrifice time
and work hard for others' sake.

The more you put in,
the more you'll get out,
the bigger the difference,
that's what it's about.

So continue to think big,
and keep an open-mind,
because it will mean the world
to all humankind.

T

USE TECHNOLOGY

In order to have your message travel far and wide,
use technology, the internet and the resources they provide.

Using limited resources, you can reach millions, you'll see,
by creating a website or using social media, both of which are free.

Spread your knowledge and action as far as you can,
to positively affect every child, woman and man.

EVALUATE

It's time to evaluate everything you have done,
the battles you've lost and the battles you've won.

Would you do anything different or would you keep things the same?
Think about who you were and who you became.

You've made a difference to others, so they can excel,
but you've improved your skills and yourself as well.

NOW WHAT?

You've already answered the question, "What?"
with everything you have learned,
and you've shown that you care, by being concerned.

You've also answered, "So what?" and "Why should we care?"
to reach equal rights and make this world more fair.

But there's one more question that you need to figure out.
"Now what?" is the question that you can't move on without.

It's time to consider what it is that comes next.
The answer may be simple, or it may be complex.

eXamine

As you take the next step,
imagine what could happen
if everyone in the world
chose to take action.

What impact would this have? What changes would occur?
How would we treat each other? Would it change who we were?

Examine your action and the change it can bring,
continue to mold it, shape it, and watch it grow wings.

An idea that began with believing that you can,
has helped make a difference, which is why we began.

YOU

It's time to appreciate all that you've done,
this journey's been difficult, but it's also been fun.

You've learned and you've grown and great friends you have made,
and in the process you've helped others and provided much aid.

Celebrate your accomplishments and thank others too.
Without them it wouldn't have happened, but it all started with you.

Y

ZEAL

You've proven your dedication and that you've got zeal,
which means an eagerness towards a cause, which is something unreal.

"A" may be for Action, but it's also for All,
one or many can act, it's up to you, it's really your call.

You can put this book down, and set it aside,
or you can use every page as your own action guide.

This A-Z guide explains the skills and the how,
so flip back to "A", why not start now?

Z

WHERE TO GET STARTED

It's time to get started! By reading this book you have already learned the steps to take action that can make a difference to and in the world.

The activities on the following pages will help you practice a few of the skills mentioned in this book.

Remember "J" is for Joining Organizations.

Below are some of the authors' favorite organizations that give people around the world a voice to make a difference. Work with a parent or teacher to explore these sites for great ideas on action!

Taking Action Organizations:

www.actiontracker.org.uk Record actions and track the impact they have on the globe.

www.causes.com Share ideas, find like-minded friends, and make an impact using this platform.

www.voicesofyouth.org Learn about issues affecting the world, voice your thoughts, communicate your ideas and tell everyone about actions that you and your friends are taking to make the world a better place.

www.tigweb.org Empower youth to engage and connect in order to shape a more inclusive, peaceful and sustainable world.

www.kidscanmakeadifference.org Kids Can Make A Difference® (KIDS), an educational program for middle- and high school students, focuses on the root causes of hunger and poverty, the people most affected, solutions, and how students can help.

Now that you have the skills and knowledge to take action, what can you do to make a difference to and in the world?

B IS FOR BELIEVING IN YOURSELF

Remember the story *The Little Engine that Could?*
What behaviors and attitudes helped the train reach the top of the mountain?

THINK!

Was there ever a time when you thought something was impossible?

What behaviors and attitudes helped you to believe in yourself?

E IS FOR EMPATHY

Put yourself in the shoes of someone in need.

THINK!

What would it be like to experience a day in their life?

_____

What types of challenges would you face?

_____

How would you feel?

_____

How is a day in their life similar and different from your own?

_____

How has this changed your perspective of others and yourself?

_____

G IS FOR GOAL-SETTING

What is your goal?

_____

_____

What will success look like when you have achieved this goal?

_____

_____

How will you reach your goal?

_____

_____

L IS FOR LISTENING

Think!

What is the difference between the words 'listen' and 'hear'?

_____

How can you become a better listener?

_____

How can you respectfully respond to differing perspectives?

_____

Extend!

Pair up with a peer.

Conduct a short interview.

Ask your partner about their talents and interests.

Now reverse roles.

Report back to the group. Share what you have learned by introducing your partner.

V IS FOR eVALUATE

Think!

PLUS+	What are some things that were successful throughout this process? What battles did you win?
MINUS-	What are some things that didn't work throughout this process? What battles did you lose?
WHAT'S NEXT?	What would you do differently next time?

CPSIA information can be obtained
at www.ICGtesting.com
Printed in the USA
LVIC040420080713
341778LV00003BA